Library of Congress Cataloging-in-Publication Data available.

ISBN 978-1-4521-6626-1

Manufactured in China.

FSC
www.fsc.org

MIX
Paper from
responsible sources
FSC™ C008047

Design by Alice Seiler and Jill Turney.
Typeset in Archer, Heisei Maru Gothic, Meltow, and Paqui.

10 9 8 7 6 5 4 3 2 1

Chronicle Books LLC
680 Second Street
San Francisco, California 94107

Chronicle Books—we see things differently.
Become part of our community at www.chroniclekids.com.

Let's Learn
Spanish

First Words for Everyone

Aurora Cacciapuoti

chronicle books · san francisco

Introduction

Welcome to *Let's Learn Spanish!*

This book will introduce you to some basic Spanish words. It's the beginning of your language-learning journey!

Spanish is the second-most-spoken language in the world. Also known as Castilian from its origins in the Castile region of Spain, Spanish is spoken all over the globe, and it is the mother tongue of around 400–450 million people.

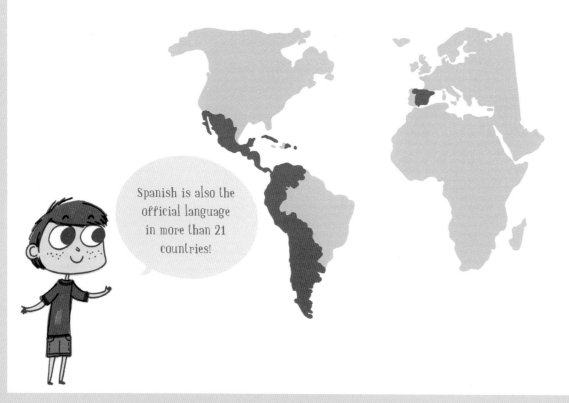

Spanish is also the official language in more than 21 countries!

Even though Spanish is spoken in so many places, there are differences between the Spanish spoken in Spain and the Spanish spoken in each Latin American country.

For example: "Hello?" when answering the phone in Spain is translated as *¿Dígame?*, but in Argentina and Bolivia it is *¿Hola?*; in Cuba it is *¿Oigo?*; in Colombia, Costa Rica, the Dominican Republic, Ecuador, El Salvador, Guatemala, Honduras, Peru, and Venezuela it is *¿Aló?*; in México it is *¿Bueno?*; and in Panama and Puerto Rico it is *¿Haló?*

¿Hola?
¿Oigo?
¿Aló?
¿Bueno?

While some words are different depending on the country, you can still communicate in different Spanish-speaking countries without difficulty using the Spanish that you know.

The Spanish words in this book focus on those spoken in North America and México.

Spanish originated from Latin, and it is a phonetic language, which means that the way the word is written is the way it is pronounced. Each letter has a precise sound.

And Spanish is a gendered language, which means that it has masculine (m) and feminine (f) words and articles. "El" is masculine singular and "los" is masculine plural. "La" is feminine singular and "las" is feminine plural. Of course, there are exceptions such as "la mano."

For example:

La sandia
(feminine singular)

Las sandias
(feminine plural)

El aguacate
(masculine singular)

Los aguacates
(masculine plural)

El maestro   La maestra

The definite article has to match the gender and number.

If you are talking about a female teacher, you would say "la maestra," while a male teacher is "el maestro." More than one female teacher would be "las maestras," while more than one male teacher would be "los maestros."

Indefinite articles are used to talk about something new or something or someone that is part of a group. For example, to say a dog—any dog—you would say, "un perro."

An indefinite article may be used to specify a quantity, such as "un beso" (a kiss) and to indicate a gender (masculine or feminine).

Masculine singular: Un   Masculine plural: Unos

Feminine singular: Una   Feminine plural: Unas

This is just the beginning of your Spanish adventure. Now, let's learn some words!

Sheep
La oveja

Cat
El gato

Chicken
La gallina

Dog
El perro

Horse
El caballo

Fish
El pez
El pescado

Deer
El venado
El ciervo

Bear
El oso

Turtle
La tortuga

Pig
El cerdo

Owl
El búho
El tecolote

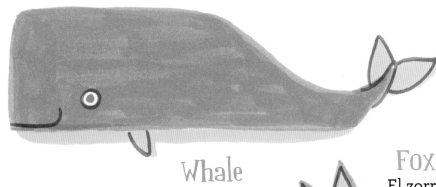

Bird
El pájaro

Whale
La ballena

Fox
El zorro

Cow
La vaca

Hair
El pelo
El cabello

Nose
La nariz

Mouth
La boca

Neck
El cuello

Leg
La pierna

Foot
El pie

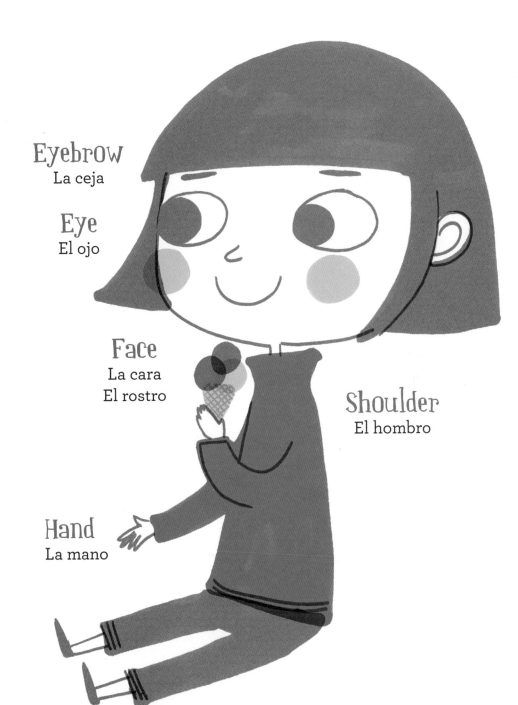

Eyebrow
La ceja

Eye
El ojo

Ear
La oreja

Face
La cara
El rostro

Shoulder
El hombro

Hand
La mano

Artichoke
La alcachofa

Carrot
La zanahoria

Pepper
El pimiento

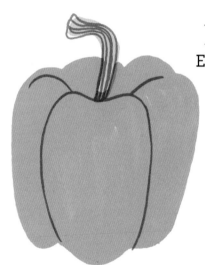

Tomato
El jitomate (red)
El tomate (green)

Garlic
El ajo

Celery
El apio

Cucumber
El pepino

Onion
La cebolla

Kale
La col rizada

Spinach
La espinaca

Potato
La papa
(Latin America)

La patata
(Spain)

Chili pepper
El chile

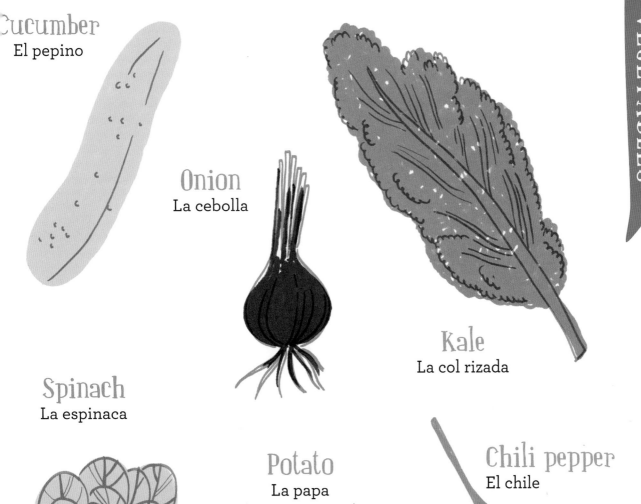

Watermelon
La sandía

Plum
La ciruela

Guava
La guayaba

Passion fruit
El/la maracuyá
(depending on country)
La granadilla

Cherry
La cereza

Bananas
Los plátanos

Pumpkin
La calabaza

Apple
La manzana

Pear
La pera

Avocado
El aguacate

Strawberry
La fresa
La frutilla
(Latin America)

Lime
El limón

Peach
El durazno
El melocotón

Orange
La naranja

Pineapple
La piña
La ananá
(Latin America)

Cheese
El queso

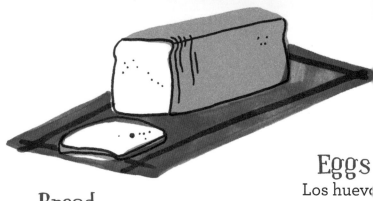

Bread
El pan

Eggs
Los huevos

Soup
La sopa
El caldo

Chicken
El pollo

Hot chocolate
El chocolate caliente

Snacks
Las botanas
Los bocadillos

Rice
El arroz

Ham
El jamón

Ice cream
El helado

Beans
Los frijoles
Las habichuelas

Corn on the cob
El elote
El choclo (Latin America)

Milk
La leche

Shrimp
El camarón

Black
Negro

Purple
Morado

Blue
Azul

Green
Verde

Yellow
Amarillo

Orang
Naran
Anaranj

Red
Rojo
Colorado

Pink
Rosa
Rosado

Brown
Marrón
Café

Gray
Gris

White
Blanco

0 **Zero**
Cero

1 **One**
Uno

2 **Two**
Dos

3 **Three**
Tres

6 **Six**
Seis

Seven
Siete 7

4

Four
Cuatro

Five
Cinco

5

Eight
Ocho

8

9

Nine
Nueve

Ten
Diez

10

Party
La fiesta

Suitcase
La maleta
El velíz

Map
El mapa

Flight
El vuelo

Ticket
El boleto
El billete (Latin America)

BOLETO
FROM: LOS ANGELES
TO: MEXICO CITY
NAME   26B   AAC

NAME
□□□□
26B □
LAX

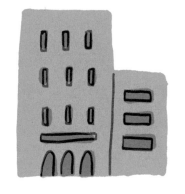

Hostel
El hostal
La residencia

Guidebook
La guía de turistas

Train station
La estación de tren

Passport
El pasaporte

Store
La tienda
El almacén

MÉXICO

PASAPORTE

Homework
La tarea

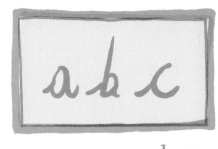

Classroom
El aula
El salón de clases

Desk
El escritorio

Student
El estudiante (m)
La estudiante (f)

Papers
Los papeles

Calendar
El calendario

Backpack
La mochila

Library
La biblioteca

Book
El libro

Pencil
El lápiz

Teacher
El profesor (m)
La profesora (f)
El maestro (m)
La maestra (f)

Bedroom
El cuarto de dormir
El dormitorio
La recámara

Lamp
La lámpara

Clock
El reloj

Pillow
La almohada
El cojín

Table
La mesa

Chair
La silla

Kitchen
La cocina

Door
La puerta

Key
La llave

Bookshelf
El estante para libros
El librero

Window
La ventana

Vase
El florero

Palm tree
La palmera

Tree
El árbol

Flowers
Las flores

Seeds
Las semillas

Soil
La tierra

Leaf
La hoja

Bee
La abeja

Sprout
El brote

Grass
El césped
El pasto (México)

Plant
La planta

Handbag
La bolsa

Shoes
Los zapatos

Hat
El sombrero

Socks
Los calcetines

Bathing suit
El traje de baño

Underwear
La ropa interior

Eyeglasses
Los anteojos
Los lentes

Scarf
La bufanda

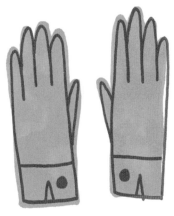

Coat
El abrigo

Gloves
Los guantes

Sweater
El suéter

Umbrella
El paraguas
La sombrilla

Nurse
El enfermero (m)
La enfermera (f)

Scientist
El científico (m)
La científica (f)

Driver
El conductor (m)
La conductora (f)

Writer
El escritor (m)
La escritora (f)

Musician
El músico (m)
La música (f)

Singer
El cantante (m)
La cantante (f)

Photographer
El fotógrafo (m)
La fotógrafa (f)

Artist
El artista (m)
La artista (f)

Cook
El cocinero (m)
La cocinera (f)

Cousin
El primo (m)   La prima (f)

Aunt
La tía

Uncle
El tío

Daughter
La hija

Moth
La ma
La ma

Grandfather
El abuelo

Father
El padre
El papá

Son
El hijo

Sister
La hermana

Brother
El hermano

Grandmother
La abuela

City
La ciudad

Mountain
La montaña
La sierra

Island
La isla

Forest
El bosque

River
El río

Theater
El teatro

Sea
El mar

House
La casa

Lake
El lago

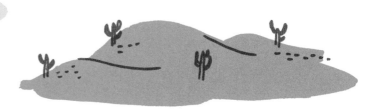

Desert
El desierto

Art museum
El museo de arte

Market
El mercado

Bus
El autobús
El camión (México)

Airplane
El avión

Car
El auto
El carro
El coche (México)

Bicycle
La bicicleta

Boat
El barco

Subway
El metro

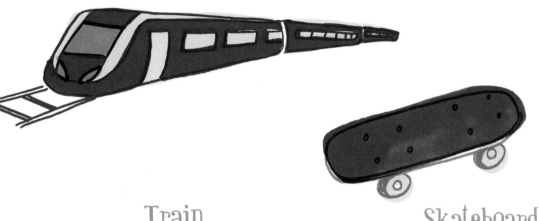

Skateboard
La patineta

Train
El tren

Truck
El camión

Motorcycle
La motocicleta

Sun
El sol

Cloud
La nube

Rain
La lluvia

Summer
El verano

Autumn
El otoño

Fog
La niebla

Wind
El viento

Snow
La nieve

Winter
El invierno

Spring
La primavera

Aurora Cacciapuoti is an author and illustrator of more than a dozen books, including *Let's Learn Japanese*. Originally from Sardinia, she lives in L'Aquila, Italy, with her husband, Armando, and her dog, Yuka.